Let's Learn
ABC

By Sachin Sachdeva

Aa

APRICOT

APPLE GOURD

ARTICHOKE

APPLE

AVOCADO

ASPARAGUS

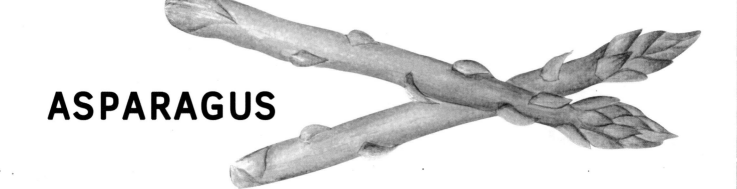

Bb

BITTER GOURD

BEANS

BLUE BERRY

BLACK BERRY

BROCCOLI

BANANA

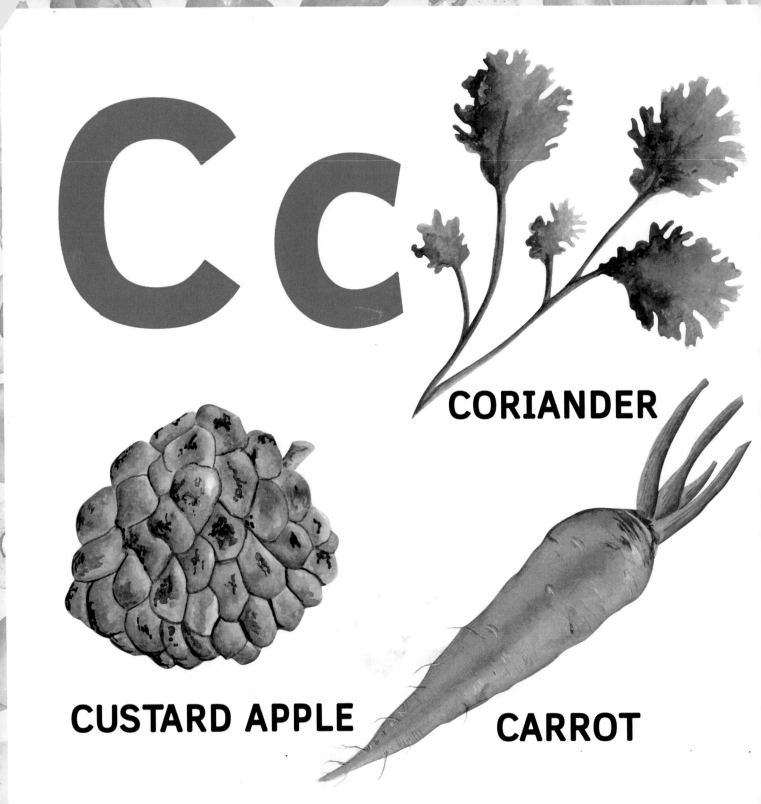

C c

CORIANDER

CUSTARD APPLE

CARROT

CHERRY

CABBAGE

CUCUMBER

Dd

DATES

DRUMSTICK

DILL

DRAGON FRUIT

Ee

EGGPLANT

ELDERBERRY

ELEPHANT FRUIT

F f

FEIJOA

FENNEL

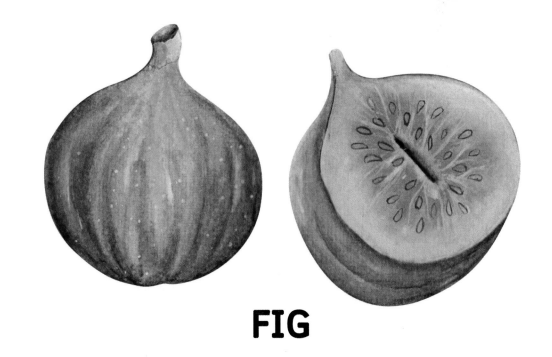

FIG

FINGER LIME

G g

GOOSEBERRY

GARLIC

GINGER

GUAVA

GRAPES

Hh

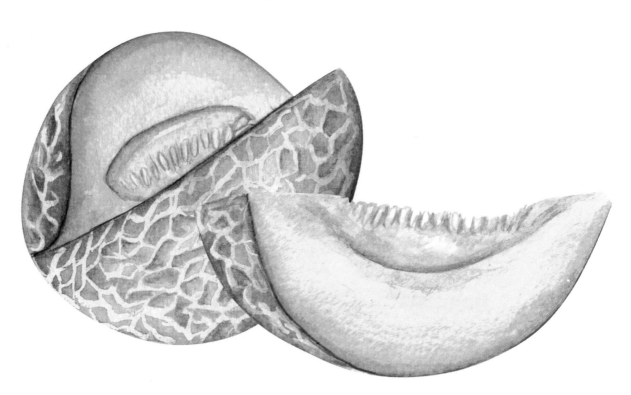

HONEYDEW MELON

HUCKLEBERRY

HORSERADISH

I i

ICEBERG LETTUCE

INDIAN JUJUBE

INDIAN PLUM

ICE APPLE

IVY GOURD

ICE CREAM BEANS

J j

JABUTICABA

JICAMA

JACKFRUIT

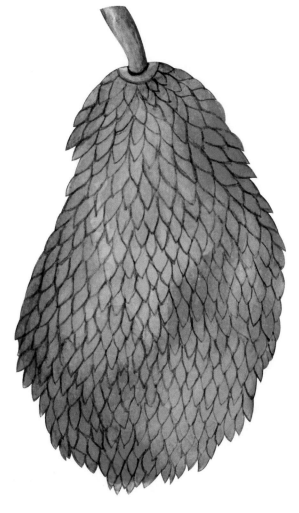

JAVAPLUM

JALAPENO

K k

KAKADU PLUM

KEI APPLE

KIWI

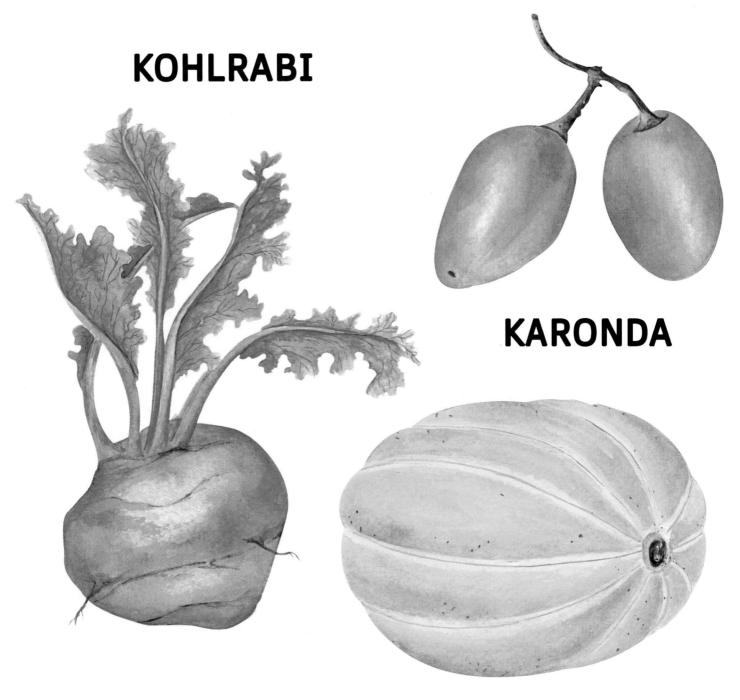

KOHLRABI

KARONDA

KOREAN MELON

L l

LOQUAT

LEMON

LYCHEE

LEEK

LOOFA GOURD

LOTUS STEM

M m

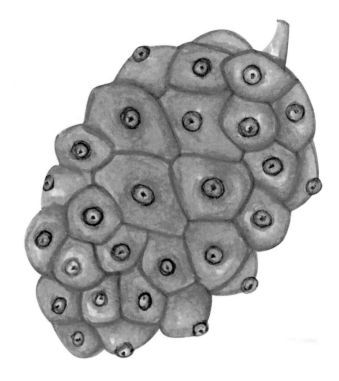

MANGOSTEEN

MORINDA

MANGO

MOMEY SAPOTE

MUSHROOM

Nn

NARANJILLA

NASHI PEAR

NOPAL

NANCE

NECTARINE

O o

ORANGE

OLIVE

ONION

OIL PLUM

OKRA

Pp

POMEGRANATE

PUMPKIN

PEAS

PEAR

PINEAPPLE

POTATO

Q q

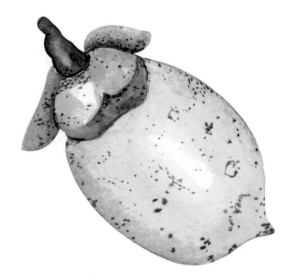

QUEEN ANNE CHERRY

QUEENSLAND EBONY

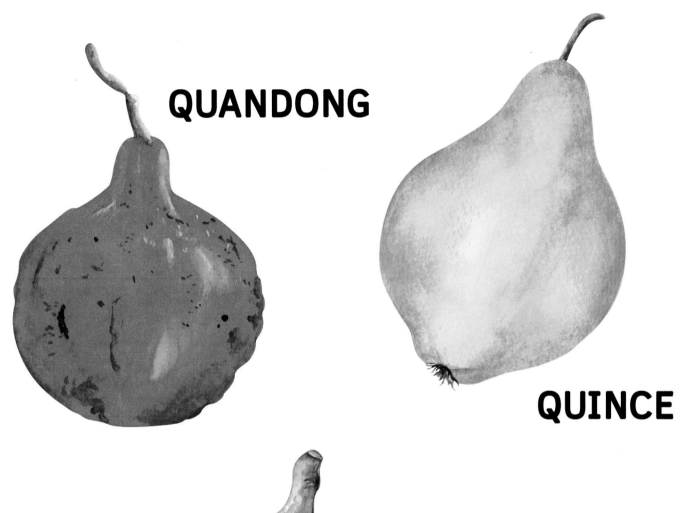

QUANDONG

QUINCE

QUARARIBEA
CORDATA

Rr

RASPBERRY

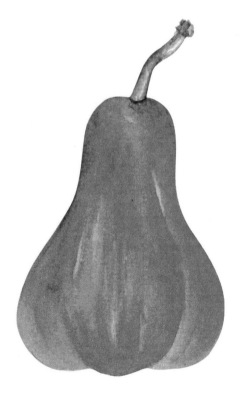

ROSE APPLE

ROUND ZUCCHINI

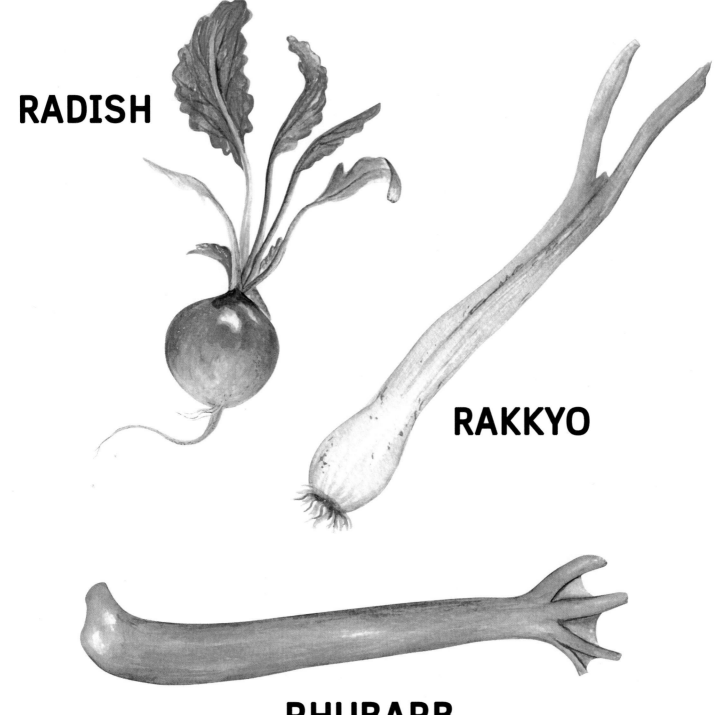

RADISH

RAKKYO

RHUBARB

S s

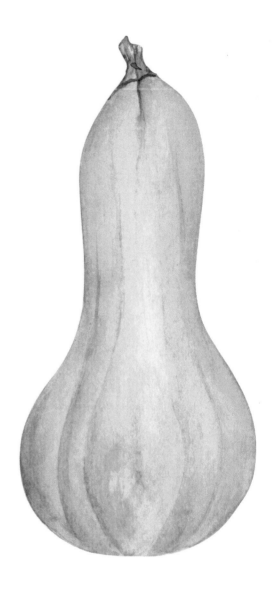

STAR APPLE

SWEET SQUASH

SAPODILLA

SWEET POTATO

STRAWBERRY

SWEET APPLE BERRY

Tt

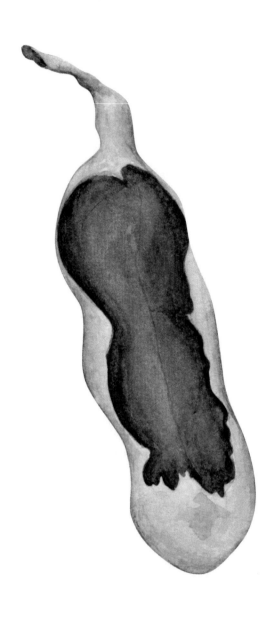

TOMATO

TAMARIND

TURNIP

TAMARILLO

TARO

U u

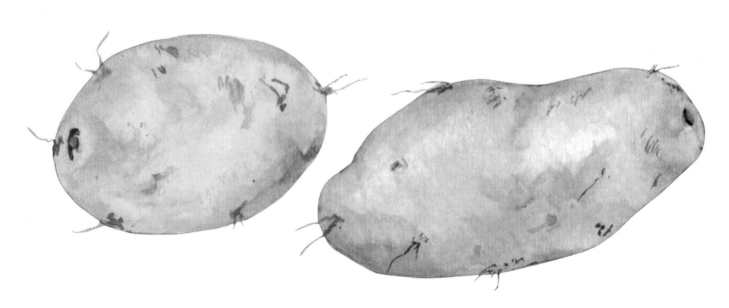

ULLUCO

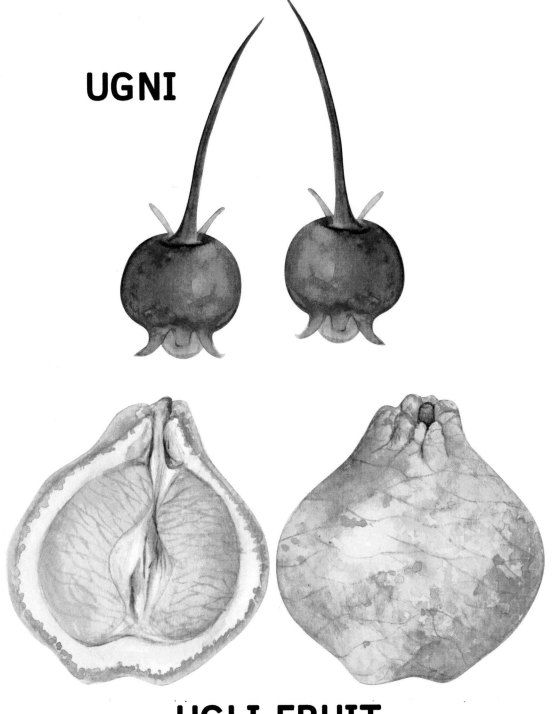

UGNI

UGLI FRUIT

V v

VELVET PINK BANANA

VOAVANGA

VELVET TAMARIND

W w

WATER CHESTNUT · WATERMELON

WOOD APPLE

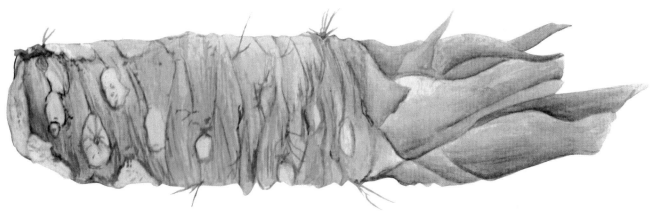

WASABI

X x

XIMENIA

XIGUA

Y y

YUMBERRY

YAM

Z z

ZUCCHINI

ZIG ZAG FRUIT

GET FIRST WORDS PICTURE BOOKS FOR YOUR CHILD
BY SACHIN SACHDEVA

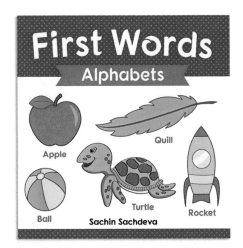

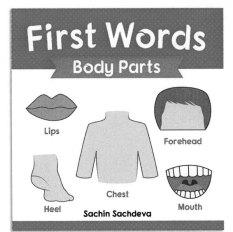

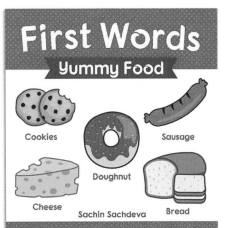

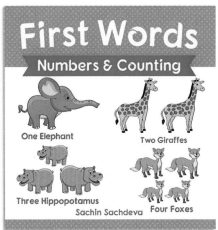

AVAILABLE ON AMAZON

Made in United States
North Haven, CT
26 January 2023

31705416R00033